Goodbye,
Fenwick
Island.
Hope to see you
soon!
annie ♡

By R. D. Rosen,
Harry Prichett &
Rob Battles

Workman
Publishing,
New York

Library of Congress Cataloging-in-
Publication Data is available.

ISBN-13: 978-0-7611-4366-6
ISBN-10: 0-7611-4366-1

Design by Paul Hanson
Layout by Patrick Borelli

Workman books are available at special
discounts when purchased in bulk for
premiums and sales promotions as well
as for fund-raising or educational use.
Special editions of book excerpts can also
be created to specification. For details,
contact the Special Sales Director at the
address below.

Workman Publishing Company, Inc.
225 Varick Street
New York, NY 10014
www.workman.com

Printed in U.S.A.
First printing July 2006

10 9 8 7 6 5 4 3 2 1

For Annie, Hannajane,
Hudson, Isabel, Lucy,
and Molly

Introduction

Being a baby's not easy.
Conditions are less than
ideal. You have negligible
motor and language skills.
You can't always get your
hands on food when you

want it. House pets are bigger than
you, often by a multiple of five or six.
Then, of course, you have parents, and
not of your own choosing. They don't
understand how rich and complicated
your emotional life is. Indeed, they
spew only nonsense syllables.

Remember what it was like? Don't
lie. If you remembered, you'd have been
hard pressed to make babies of your
own. Thanks to the blissful collective
amnesia that renders early childhood
a blur of relatives' faces and bathroom
emergencies, most

babies sail
blithely off
toward adulthood,
a stage of life
when they
themselves will
start cooing and
ooohing and

aaahing over babies. Why? Because they have *completely repressed what it's like to be one.*

Well, look what the stork just brought: Two-hundred-and-forty-some-odd tots to remind you that babies have a lot more on their minds than where their next baba is coming from. Each photo in this book features a refreshingly churlish cherub. A little devil in diapers. A precious bundle of candor, ingratitude, and . . . okay, sheer joy.

So, turn the page and watch out for drool. And none of that kitchy-kitchy-koo stuff.

--R. D. Rosen
   Harry Prichett
   Rob Battles

"I'm going for the record: 48 hours without sleep."

NAME: August

FUTURE PLANS: Opening a chain of coffee bars in day care centers

"This is really good duck!"

NAME: Sam

FUTURE PLANS: Hitchhiking through northeast Delaware

BAD BABY
EARLY WARNING SIGN #744

Baby can't stop telling
same dirty joke over and
over again.

"I'm two weeks old and already I can't stand watching Miami's offense."

NAME: Christian

FUTURE PLANS: Fighting for better pay for jurors

"I can't begin to tell you
how fantastic that was."

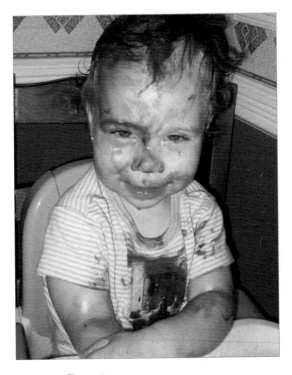

NAME: Peyton
FUTURE PLANS: Becoming a
hot buffet supervisor

"Tell me when Aunt
Barbara leaves."

NAME: Olivia
FUTURE PLANS: Promoting
lemony freshness

"It's true! I weigh three pounds less in a clean diaper!"

NAME: Josh

FUTURE PLANS: Buying in bulk

"Can you hear me now?"

NAMES: Sophie and Katya

FUTURE PLANS: Letting magazines pile up unread; becoming a speech therapist

BAD BABY
EARLY WARNING SIGN #132

Baby refuses to shoot chariot race scene in day care production of *Ben Hur*.

"The only reason I make these cute faces is so you'll support me until I'm 37."

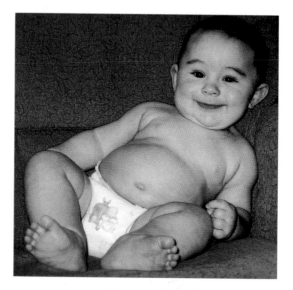

NAME: Brandon

FUTURE PLANS: Never buying health insurance

"Put your hand down.
This is not a real parade,
and you're not running
for office."

NAMES: Matt and Molly
FUTURE PLANS: Making empty
campaign promises;
starting a union for
whistleblowers

**BAD BABY
EARLY WARNING SIGN #209**

Baby is horrified to
discover that favorite
food-encrusted pacifier
has been washed.

"Oopsy! Another poopsy!"

NAME: Delaney
FUTURE PLANS: Developing
sports drinks for the
sedentary

"I hate how sloppy Jesse gets with a coupla juice boxes in him."

NAMES: Jesse and Misaki
FUTURE PLANS: Rethinking the whole man-woman thing

"Merciful God, if she winds up that musical mobile one more time, my head's going to implode."

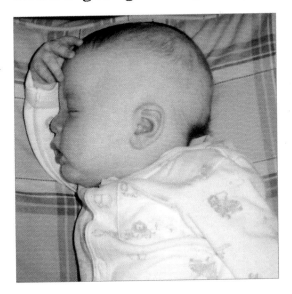

NAME: Kieran
FUTURE PLANS: Becoming a monastery consultant

BAD BABY
EARLY WARNING SIGN #525

Baby refuses
to let go of
Village
People
obsession.

"Schotzy's doing her best, but someday I want to find my birth mother."

NAME: Jon
FUTURE PLANS: Creating a line of vegan German foods

BAD BABY
EARLY WARNING SIGN #75

Baby won't stop reporting
imaginary Thanksgiving
Day parade.

NAME: Molly
FUTURE PLANS: Disappointing my mother repeatedly

"All I said was that I
was going to turn her
into an iguana."

NAMES: Olivia and Sophia
FUTURE PLANS: Googling my
coworkers; spending my
20s getting tattooed

BAD BABY
EARLY WARNING SIGN #450

Baby demands negatives,
or else promises to
destroy Dad's camera.

"You have to be in a certain state of mind to appreciate Hendrix."

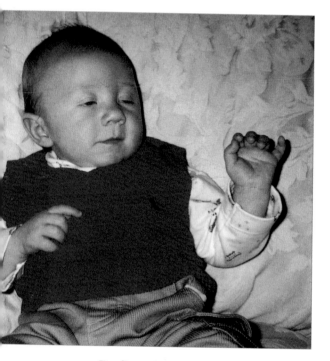

NAME: Dylan
FUTURE PLANS: Surfing the Internet in my Speedo

"Here's one thing they'll never say about me: 'plays well with others.'"

NAME: Vincent

FUTURE PLANS: Running a multinational candy company

"Try and flush it now."

NAME: Lauren

FUTURE PLANS: Raising
Akitas in Vermont

"I'm having a mashed yam flashback!"

NAME: Sophia

FUTURE PLANS: Finding a comfortable pair of pants

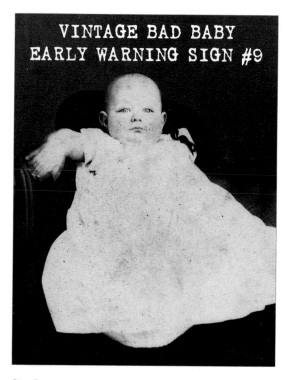

VINTAGE BAD BABY
EARLY WARNING SIGN #9

Baby refuses to move
until the turn of the
century.

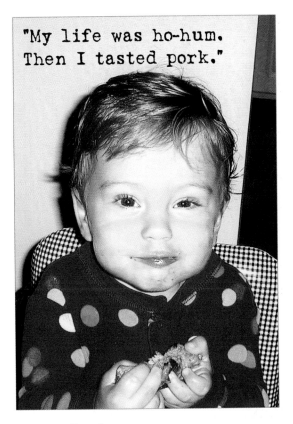

"My life was ho-hum. Then I tasted pork."

NAME: Jack

FUTURE PLANS: Opening Jack's Ribs and Bibs

VINTAGE BAD BABY
"Finley, get my checkbook and let's go shopping."

NAME: Catherine

FUTURE PLANS: Switching brokers frequently

BAD BABY
EARLY WARNING SIGN #480

Baby joins Teamsters
before he can sit up.

VINTAGE BAD BABY

"Finley, find out who
owns this building.
And buy it."

NAME: Catherine

FUTURE PLANS: Switching
analysts frequently

"Mommy, I think this guy's Jewish."

NAME: Harry

FUTURE PLANS: Telling strangers they have something in their teeth

VINTAGE BAD BABY

"I like this park, Finley.
Buy it. And all the people
in it."

NAME: Catherine

FUTURE PLANS: Finding the
perfect finials for my
lamps.

BAD BABY
EARLY WARNING SIGN #480

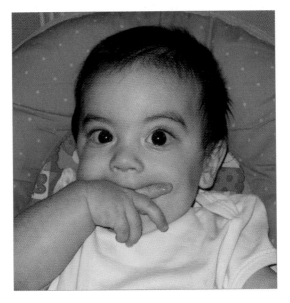

Baby already concocting
scheme to have older
brother sent to foster
home.

"Sometimes, when I think of all the babies without hair, I feel sad."

NAME: Tai
FUTURE PLANS: Operating a hair donor clinic

BAD BABY
EARLY WARNING SIGN #127

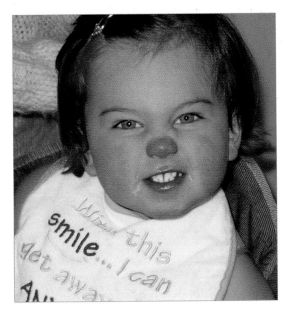

Baby turns up nose at
slightest mention of
mixed vegetables.

"This is what I think of your nap."

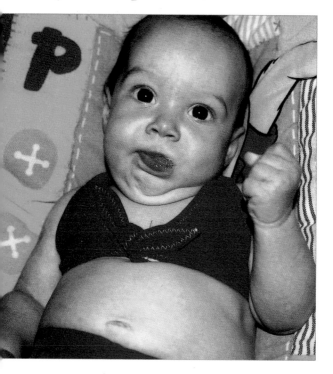

NAME: Baleigh
FUTURE PLANS: Working on upper body strength

"I don't know why I find it so funny when you get gas, Jack, but I just do."

NAMES: Jack and Abbey
FUTURE PLANS: Steering clear of cabbage; visiting Peru

"Let's hit the blackjack table, Dad--I'm really feeling it."

NAME: Charlene

FUTURE PLANS: Designing a gambling shoe

"You're very tense. You've been playing too hard. Tomorrow, let's just spend the day teething."

NAMES: Avery and Alice

FUTURE PLANS: Being a blender tester; making a difference in the lives of six-year-olds

"Mom? The baby faces?
Bor-ring."

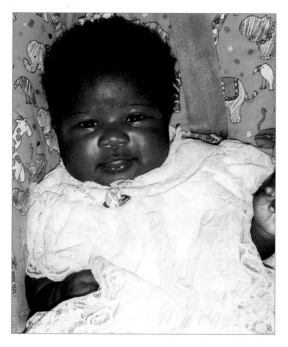

NAME: Monica
FUTURE PLANS: Plumbing the
mysteries of cheese
production

BAD BABY
EARLY WARNING SIGN #14

Baby insists on driving
with one eye closed.

DAILY AFFIRMATION

"Today I will stop
watching tornado
specials on The Weather
Channel."

--*Lucas*

BAD BABY
EARLY WARNING SIGN #45

Baby hypnotizes stuffed
bear, then forgets to
wake him up.

"I've got my mom's eyes and my dad's comb-over."

NAME: Michael

FUTURE PLANS: Putting off my first colonoscopy as long as possible

"Hey Dad, get your big butt over here and give me a push."

NAME: Paul
FUTURE PLANS: Developing a terry cloth fetish

"Get a damn dog already."

NAME: Matthew

FUTURE PLANS: Saying
"I could do that" but
never doing it

BAD BABY
EARLY WARNING SIGN #495

Baby refuses to get help
for compulsive shopping.

"Lean to the left,
Lean to the right,
I'm going to scream
In my crib all night."

NAME: Kayla
FUTURE PLANS: Rooting for
any team that provides a
pleated skirt

"I'm sorry. I didn't catch that. The thermometer goes *where*?"

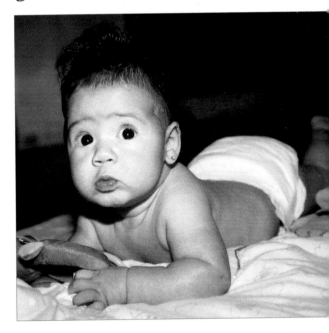

NAME: Rosie

FUTURE PLANS: Watching my cholesterol too closely

"Looks like another long night of pickled eggs and Slim Jims."

NAME: Simon

FUTURE PLANS: Running on a platform of traditional family values while cheating on my wife

BAD BABY
EARLY WARNING SIGN #928

Baby spends too much
time contemplating
destruction of universe.

"I picked him up at day care."

NAME: Wesley

FUTURE PLANS: Developing artificial gills for aging sea bass

"Let's give it up for all the nannies, and make sure you try the rice cakes."

NAME: Charlie
FUTURE PLANS: Writing jingles for paper products

"Everyone loves my corn-
and-booger muffins."

NAME: Alexander

FUTURE PLANS: Catering pet
parties

"For crying out loud, Mom--will ya stop buying me shoes from Payless? They're killin' me."

NAME: Trish
FUTURE PLANS: Trying to guess people's PIN numbers

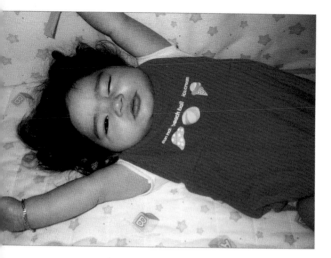

"Ah--I'm refreshed and ready for a few hours of high-pitched shrieking."

NAME: Rachael

FUTURE PLANS: Singing in an annoying falsetto after being told not to

"Those Similac shooters
really creep up on you."

NAMES: Rita and Cliff

FUTURE PLANS: Exaggerating
our own accomplishments,
no matter how small

VINTAGE BAD BABY
EARLY WARNING SIGN #37

Baby insists family bob
for him on Halloween.

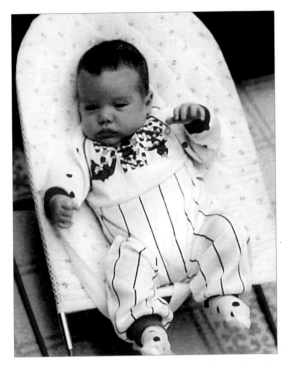

"I'm a Yankee *doody* dandy."

NAME: Mark
FUTURE PLANS: Creating a
Web site for lovers of
osso buco

BAD BABY
EARLY WARNING SIGN #48

Baby wants to continue
staring contest late into
the night.

"You want savings? You want bargains?? Crawl on all fours if you have to, but come on down to Droolin' Dave's Used Blankets, Booties & Bedding!"

NAME: Droolin' Dave

FUTURE PLANS: Avoiding jail time

BAD BABY
EARLY WARNING SIGN #700

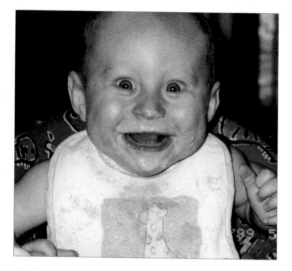

Baby too easily excited
by sight of favorite
babysitter.

BAD BABY
EARLY WARNING SIGN #708

Baby shows early
indications of road rage.

"What I love about christenings is the all-you-can-eat pablum buffet."

NAME: Amaya

FUTURE PLANS: Talking on the phone day and night

"Dear Lord, please make Grandpa put his shirt back on."

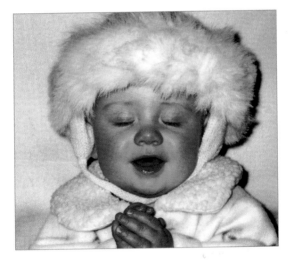

NAME: Alyssa

FUTURE PLANS: Founding a religion based on clothing

MIAMI--
Donny "The Dopp Kit"
Randall tries to smuggle
used rubber nipples into
South America.

"Me and the baby want to renegotiate the parent-child relationship."

NAMES: Sydney and Leslie

FUTURE PLANS: Wearing shoes without Velcro; making a lot of money and then making a lot more money

BAD BABY
EARLY WARNING SIGN #658

Baby thinks it's funny to
pull out Grandpa's nose
hairs.

"You're now asleep. When you awake, it is you who will be blamed for everything."

NAMES: Maggie and Peyton
FUTURE PLANS: Entertaining on cruise ships

"Don't make me get out of this high chair and come over there!"

NAME: Sophia

FUTURE PLANS: Working as a bouncer at Chuck E. Cheese's

BAD BABY
EARLY WARNING SIGN #44

Baby has uncanny knack
for finding Granny's
vodka.

"What is this crap?"

NAME: Olivia
FUTURE PLANS: Watching TV
until my brain rots

"You'll want to wash these again."

NAME: Hasan

FUTURE PLANS: Pioneering stain reduction therapy

BAD BABY
EARLY WARNING SIGN #784

Baby makes light of
mother's allergy to
shellfish.

"Shhh, here she comes.
I'll take the right one,
you take the left."

NAMES: Chris and Scott
FUTURE PLANS: Archiving
variety shows from the
late forties

BAD BABY
EARLY WARNING SIGN #317

Baby practices insincere
smile for later in life.

"You know that slogan, 'Just do it?' I just did."

NAME: Chelsea

FUTURE PLANS: Walking a fine line between avant-garde and self-indulgent

VINTAGE BAD BABY

"Bedtime? You're kidding, right?"

NAME: Stu

FUTURE PLANS: Using hair replacement products before I even start balding

Baby can't get enough of
Elton John.

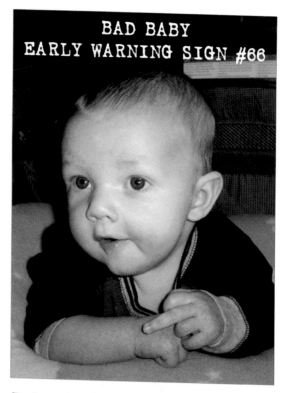

BAD BABY
EARLY WARNING SIGN #66

Baby indicates
displeasure with
Dad's tone of voice.

"And now, 'Melancholy Baby' on butt trumpet!"

NAME: Sophie
FUTURE PLANS: Designing wind instruments

"If I have to listen to another of Grandpa's hard-luck stories about wearing hand-me-downs, I'm going to vomit."

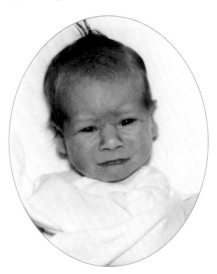

NAME: Chrissy

FUTURE PLANS: Selling off Mother's good silver a piece at a time

"Wait'll he starts talking about the eight-mile walk to school without shoes-- I'm praying for mumps."

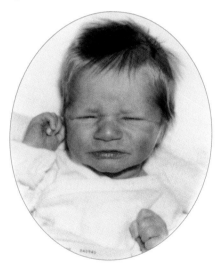

NAME: Michael
FUTURE PLANS: Secretly dipping dad's dental floss in the toilet

BAD BABY
EARLY WARNING SIGN #843

Babies respond to Disney
songs with marked
skepticism.

"Hey, baby. Like my crib?"

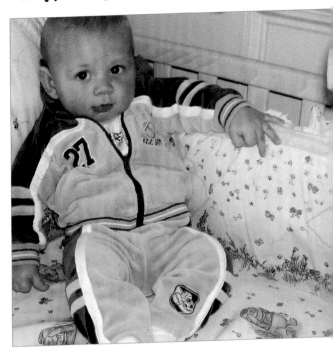

NAME: Matthew
FUTURE PLANS: Being a
distributor for Harveys
Bristol Cream

"We're excited to show you our collection."

NAMES: Sean and Kyle
FUTURE PLANS: Curating an exhibit of early American latrines

BAD BABY
EARLY WARNING SIGN #692

Baby calls moratorium on
consumption of prunes.

"I got whatever ya need,
kid--binkies, rattles,
primo Similac . . .

NAME: Scott
FUTURE PLANS: Running a
roadside topiary
attraction

BAD BABY
EARLY WARNING SIGN #5

Baby uses telekinesis to
transport grandparents
back to Sarasota.

"Got snot?"

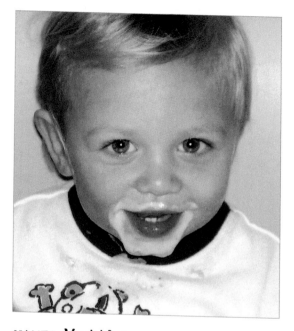

NAME: Matthew
FUTURE PLANS: Running
every idea up the
flagpole

"Stop the madness, Mom!
No more puréed clams
casino!"

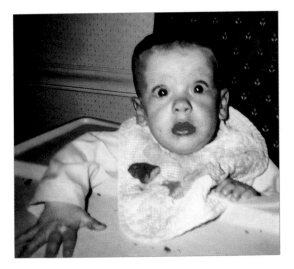

NAME: Adam

FUTURE PLANS: Buying at
least one Motor Trend
Car of the Year

"You guys go on ahead.
I gotta take care of a
little business."

NAME: Harry

FUTURE PLANS: Becoming a
national park ranger

BAD BABY
EARLY WARNING SIGN #387

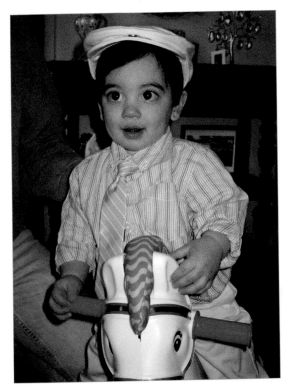

Baby loses college
tuition fund at Hialeah.

"I'm going to slip into something dry. Help yourself to a chilled binky."

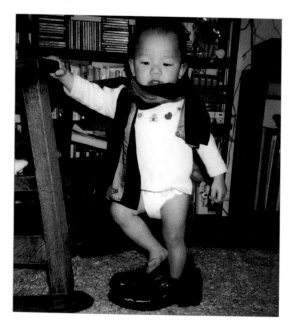

NAME: Shulian

FUTURE PLANS: Waging war on apathy

NAPERVILLE--
The Baxter Brothers are
too tired to follow
through on bank heist.

VINTAGE BAD BABY

"See that mom sitting behind me? She'll nurse anyone."

NAMES: Jonathan and Jordin

FUTURE PLANS: Mourning microfiche; designing platform shoes for toddlers

BAD BABY
EARLY WARNING SIGN #462

Children bore parents
with five-hour
performance art piece.

VINTAGE BAD BABY

"What do you mean, there's nothing funny about the Depression?"

NAME: Hildegaarde
FUTURE PLANS: Creating my own dust bowls

"Great! And it's only eight days till my circumcision."

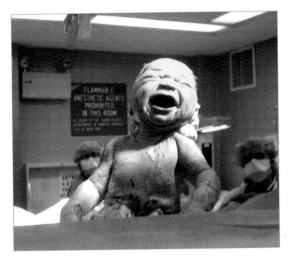

NAME: Jack
FUTURE PLANS: Getting vaccinations, tetanus shot, root canal, colonoscopy

"The hardest part about traveling alone at my age is meeting other babies."

NAME: Alondra

FUTURE PLANS: Working from home

BAD BABY
EARLY WARNING SIGN #82

Baby threatens to go into
vaudeville and ruin the
family name.

"You know what, Uncle Ted? In all the time I've known you, I've never laughed at one of your jokes."

NAME: John

FUTURE PLANS: Playing tricks on college cheerleaders

"Remember, only you can prevent diaper fires."

NAME: Alex
FUTURE PLANS: Running FEMA

BAD BABY
EARLY WARNING SIGN #958

Baby intentionally
offends grandparents
during Hanukkah.

"Isn't it funny to think about how little we have in common, and yet we have to be involved for the rest of our lives?"

NAME: Hannah
FUTURE PLANS: Rewriting Joni Mitchell's lyrics

"I've got to get away from this crazy family."

NAME: Spencer
FUTURE PLANS: Putting Freud back on top

"I'm in the *wetness* protection program."

NAME: Danny Big Thighs

FUTURE PLANS: Avoiding the insidious pull of nostalgia

"Got-ta poop! Got-ta poop!"

NAME: Matthew

FUTURE PLANS: Managing bodily-function novelty acts

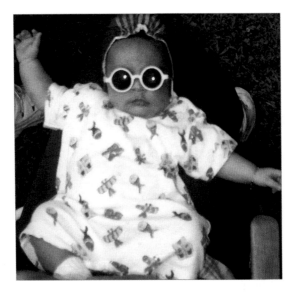

"Marvin! Get our guests some fresh breast milk!"

NAME: Marva

FUTURE PLANS: Discovering a better holiday meat than turkey

BAD BABY
EARLY WARNING SIGN #591

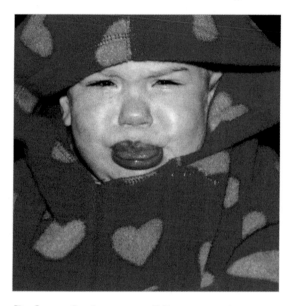

Baby feigns allergy to
fleece to obtain designer
outerwear.

"Just because you're my parents doesn't mean I'm not profiling you."

NAME: James
FUTURE PLANS: Eating powdered donuts

"They used to laugh at me. Now I have my own pool."

NAME: Daniel

FUTURE PLANS: Driving former friends into bankruptcy

"Fooled you! I'm not cooking risotto!"

NAME: Paige
FUTURE PLANS: Writing a restaurant column for a rural weekly newspaper

"Not to worry. The tide will take it out."

NAME: Steven

FUTURE PLANS: Being a stickler about use of "that" and "which"

DAILY AFFIRMATION

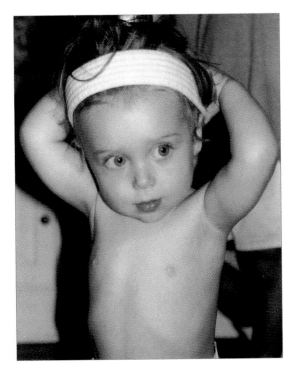

"Today I will start using
a longer-lasting
underarm deodorant."
                    --Lena

"Jake, I had no *idea* you were Jewish!"

NAMES: Lily and Jake
FUTURE PLANS: Investigating investigative reporters; celebrating the winter solstice in May

MASSAPEQUA PARK--
Julia Sore Gums is
arrested for running
interstate teething ring.

VINTAGE BAD BABY
EARLY WARNING SIGN #67

Lester perfects vacant TV
stare 27 years prior to
invention of TV.

"You read these things,
it makes you not want to
go anywhere."

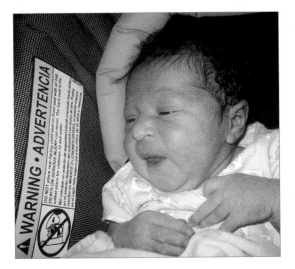

NAME: Keila

FUTURE PLANS: Obsessing
about former babysitters

"This will be perfect on the new drapes."

NAME: Stephanie

FUTURE PLANS: Driving with left turn signal on

BAD BABY
EARLY WARNING SIGN #369

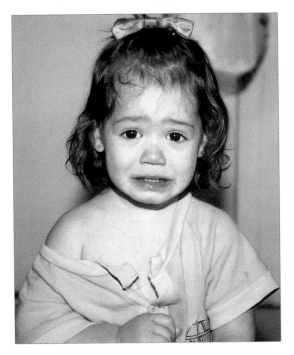

Baby won't stop reciting
monologue from *Who's
Afraid of Virginia Woolf?*

"Guess where my hand's been."

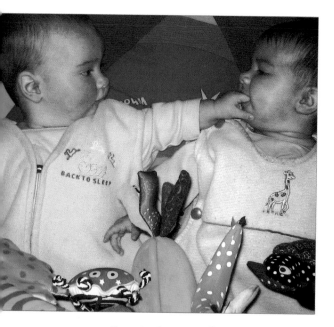

NAMES: Sophie and Katya

FUTURE PLANS: Developing game shows; avoiding all human contact

BAD BABY
EARLY WARNING SIGN #916

Baby gets part-time job
playing Playskool piano
in neighborhood lounge.

"You tell me. Gorgonzola
or Roquefort?"

NAME: Ian

FUTURE PLANS: Practicing
laproscopic surgery
without a medical license

BAD BABY
EARLY WARNING SIGN #207

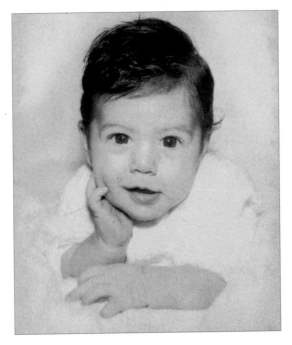

Baby already scheming to
get trust money early.

"Observe, Mom. I'm going to show you the way to do this."

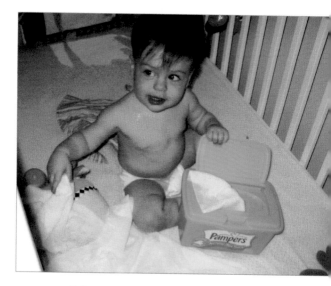

NAME: Simon

FUTURE PLANS: Sharing computer viruses with classmates

"I'm tired of this lifestyle. I'm ready for a meaningful relationship."

NAME: Lucio

FUTURE PLANS: Finding a swingers support group

"Oh, hey, Dad. I was just telling Jennifer about how you met Mom when you were working on the docks."

NAMES: Christine and Jennifer

FUTURE PLANS: Not letting boyfriends know which one of us they're dating

"Manuel, massage please.
My legs are tense."

NAME: **Justine**
FUTURE PLANS: **Never leaving
Florida**

"I fart like a butterfly and stink like a bee."

NAME: Gabriella

FUTURE PLANS: Taking the guesswork out of bill paying

"I can no longer pretend
I enjoy Grandpa John's
pathetic pony rides."

NAME: Eunice

FUTURE PLANS: Getting
multiple advanced
degrees

VINTAGE BAD BABY
EARLY WARNING SIGN #12

Baby uses oversize
dressing gown to smuggle
Swedish au pair into
country.

"Gee Willikers, she can really fill a diaper."

NAME: William
FUTURE PLANS: Poultry inspector

"I got one. A nanny, a one-year-old, and a priest walk into a day care center. . . ."

NAME: Theo
FUTURE PLANS: Making inappropriate comments at funerals

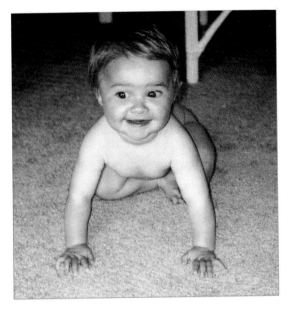

"Guess which one is puppy's and which is mine?"

NAME: Sara

FUTURE PLANS: Hosting interactive psychic hotline

BAD BABY
EARLY WARNING SIGN #361

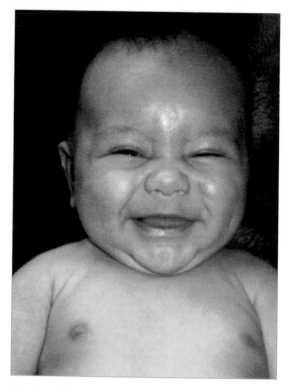

Baby laughs even though
he doesn't "get" joke.

"Yo! Adrian!"

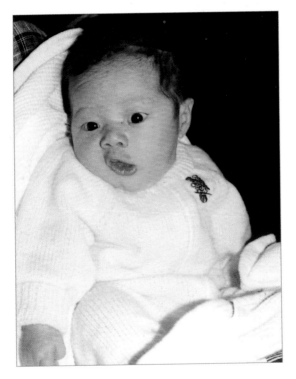

NAME: Lein

FUTURE PLANS: Drinking raw
eggs

"Behold! With this lollipop, I now embark on a lifelong journey of tooth-rotting candy consumption."

NAME: Brooklyn

FUTURE PLANS: Writing a book about nougat

BAD BABY
EARLY WARNING SIGN #427

Babies won't stop singing
Captain & Tennille's
greatest hits.

"You won't be needing to pay the sitter."

NAME: Kimberley
FUTURE PLANS: Sabotaging my career with angry outbursts

"The snoring, the smell, the fidgeting--please take her away."

NAMES: Keila and Karen

FUTURE PLANS: Inventing two useless kitchen gadgets

BAD BABY
EARLY WARNING SIGN #38

Baby agrees to play Vegas for scale.

"These expired juice boxes have quite a kick!"

NAME: Caroline

FUTURE PLANS: Repeating sophomore year--twice

BAD BABY
EARLY WARNING SIGN #85

Baby figures out way to
punish cat by playing
Metallica at high volume.

TARZANA, CALIFORNIA--
Steven Vago hires union
goons to shut down day
care center until Fig
Newtons are taken off
menu.

"Yeah, baby! I beat the point spread!"

NAME: Drew

FUTURE PLANS: Never relaxing, even with a month off

"You call this a crib?
You cheap bums."

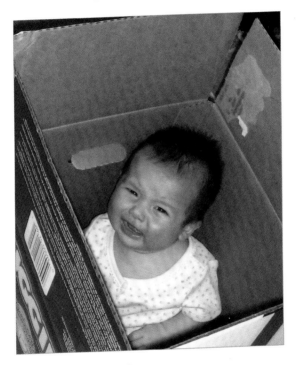

NAME: Misaki

FUTURE PLANS: Horning in on focus groups

"This actually tastes better when it comes back up."

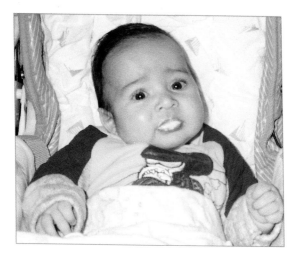

NAME: Michael

FUTURE PLANS: Delivering bad news with a cheerful expression

BAD BABY
EARLY WARNING SIGN #647

Baby can't stop
ruminating about
childhood.

"That hurts me, Mom. That hurts when you say I'm stinky."

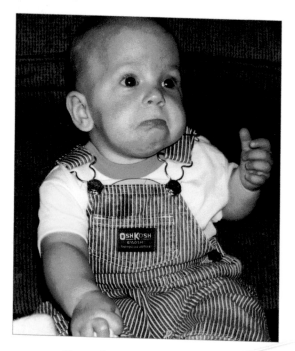

NAME: Darion

FUTURE PLANS: Becoming a public defender

"Wait till Santa sees what *I* left *him* in the fireplace."

NAME: Amaya

FUTURE PLANS: Punking more holiday icons

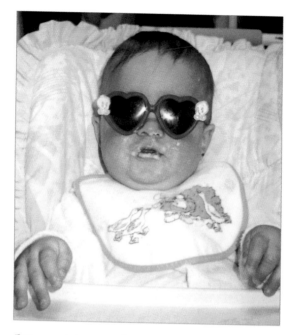

"I gotta tell you, Frank,
early retirement's not
what it's cracked up to be."

NAME: Christine

FUTURE PLANS: Figuring out
what "401K" means

"These all-night nursing parties are killin' me."

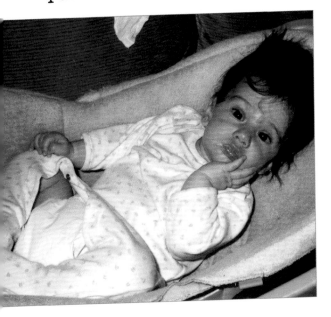

NAME: Sam
FUTURE PLANS: Idolizing worthless celebrities

BAD BABY
EARLY WARNING SIGN #108

Baby does dinner dishes
in dirty bath water.

"I'm so excited about our next guest, I think I wet myself."

NAME: Dharma

FUTURE PLANS: Syndicating myself to other planets

"Let's take it from the top--and, Grandma, you're coming in a little early on the English muffin."

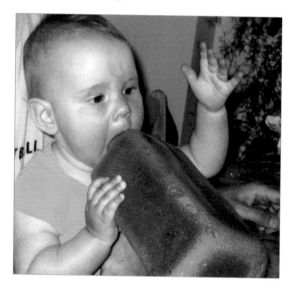

NAME: Gabrielle
FUTURE PLANS: Following other people's dreams

"Gee, Mom, they both look so good I don't know where to start."

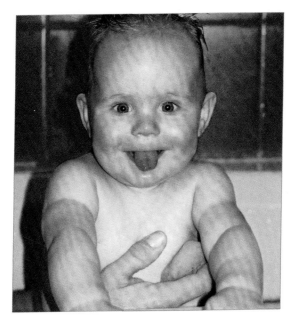

NAME: JohnRobert
FUTURE PLANS: Inventing self-unpacking luggage

BAD BABY
EARLY WARNING SIGN #676

Eggs on bickering parents.

"My brother says he learned this from a Jean Claude Van Damme movie."

NAME: Alex

FUTURE PLANS: Operating a chain of Belgian waffle restaurants

"Will ya shut your piehole, Kermie! We're trying to watch the game."

NAME: Michael
FUTURE PLANS: Meeting Steve Sabol of NFL Films

BAD BABY
EARLY WARNING SIGN #365

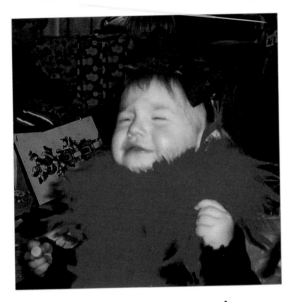

Baby won't stop praying
for little sister to go
back to hospital.

"Someone's crying, My Lord"--everybody now-- "Kumbaya."

NAME: Stephanie
FUTURE PLANS: Perfecting my zydeco dance moves

BAD BABY
EARLY WARNING SIGN #155

Baby mocks mother's
heartfelt diary entries.

"The worst thing about Halloween is sleeping off the candy corn."

NAME: Michael

FUTURE PLANS: Developing a stomach pump that can be used by children

BAD BABY
EARLY WARNING SIGN #830

Baby won't stop directing
imaginary traffic.

"Wow, you really outdid yourself, Mom."

NAME: Charlotte

FUTURE PLANS: Wasting my vote every four years

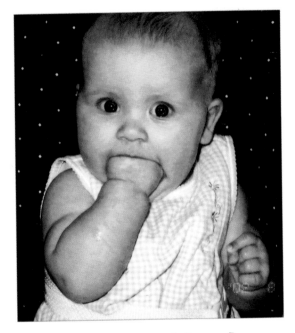

"Mumf famma wahlum."

NAME: Numum

FUTURE PLANS: Famma fo

Baby feigns sleep to avoid performing as Tevya in *Toddler on the Roof.*

HOUSTON--
Ray Edwards is arrested
on fraud charges for
trumped-up mileage
claims for his coin-
operated car.

"When I get outta here,
you're toast."

NAME: John
FUTURE PLANS: Avoiding
clutter at all costs

BAD BABY EARLY WARNING
SIGN #303

Baby pummels plush toy
for getting too close to
Halloween candy.

"You take a nap."

NAME: Luke

FUTURE PLANS: Becoming the parking-lot king of Casper, Wyoming

"To be honest, Jake,
nobody wants to work
with a leading man who's
not toilet trained."

NAME: Olivia
FUTURE PLANS: Exploiting
the little guy

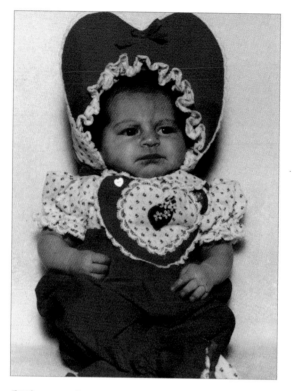

"I'm a love machine."

NAME: Kayla

FUTURE PLANS: Learning to establish boundaries

BAD BABY
EARLY WARNING SIGN #869

Baby's happiness is
nothing more than cheap
theatrics.

"Don't try to stop me--I've put up with you for eleven months."

NAME: Gabriella
FUTURE PLANS: Refusing to yield to despair

BAD BABY
EARLY WARNING SIGN #74

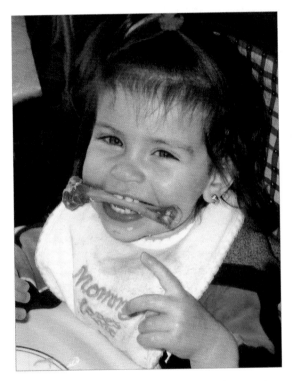

Baby taunts vegetarian aunt.

"So I says to him, 'Beat my sales numbers, *then* tell me about my drinking.'"

NAME: Kristi

FUTURE PLANS: Getting more and more bang for the buck

"We're going to the swing now, see? And you're gonna push me as long as I feel like it, understand?"

NAME: Annie

FUTURE PLANS: Performing a one-woman tribute to Shecky Green

BAD BABY
EARLY WARNING SIGN #94

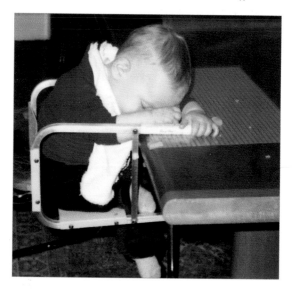

Baby overdramatizes
hunger pangs.

"Hey, Ben, how about another cold frosty teething toy?"

NAME: Alexander

FUTURE PLANS: Being an incredibly loyal friend to 15 people

"Call the warden.
I'm ready to talk."

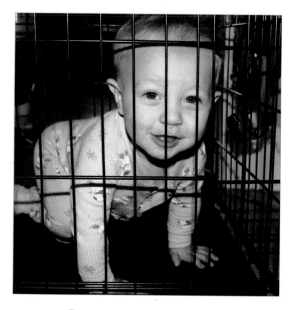

NAME: Jesse

FUTURE PLANS: Not talking
about what happened in
cell block C

"I'll pout if I want to. I don't care *who's* coming to town."

NAME: Riley

FUTURE PLANS: Looking constantly for my reading glasses

LONDON--
Jiggs Wentworth III
tries to crash royal
reception wearing crude
two-dimensional disguise.

"The duck and I need to be alone."

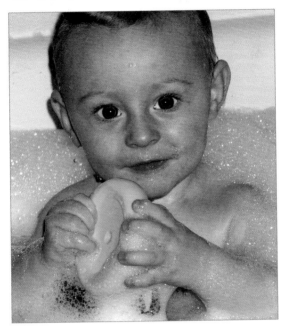

NAME: Chris
FUTURE PLANS: Designing hood ornaments

"And now, a loving tribute to my high-fiber breakfast."

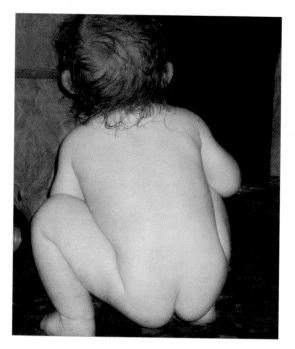

NAME: Rubin

FUTURE PLANS: Interior decorator

VINTAGE BAD BABIES

"Okay, Al. You take the nine-to-one shift, I'll do the one-to-five, and we'll keep 'em both up all night."

NAMES: Alan and Edward

FUTURE PLANS: Submitting each other's urine samples

BAD BABY
EARLY WARNING SIGN #914

Baby pretends to be
middle-aged Lebanese
character actor whenever
Grandma comes over.

"When the onesie's on my head, it means there's a twosie in my diaper."

NAME: Sofia

FUTURE PLANS: Starting for Argentina's World Cup Soccer Team

"I have no idea who took your barbecue sauce."

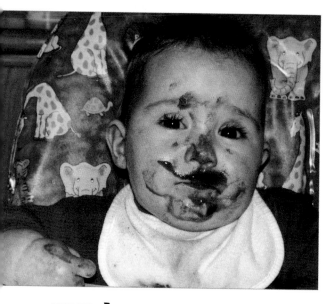

NAME: Lauren
FUTURE PLANS: Denying the existence of the 17th century

DAILY AFFIRMATION
"Today I'll stop being so
nauseatingly cute."
                                    --Akolbia

"Here's what I think of your suggestion that I behave like a big boy."

NAME: Parker

FUTURE PLANS: Decorating my entire house like a college dorm

"This is an exclusive club. Bed-wetters only. Can I see some ID?"

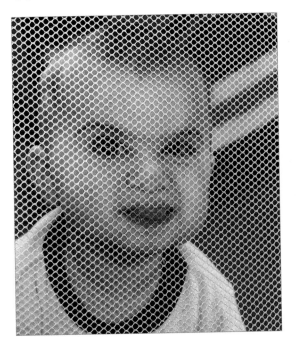

NAME: J.T.
FUTURE PLANS: Remarking on other people's weight

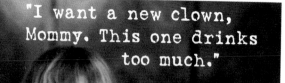

"I want a new clown, Mommy. This one drinks too much."

NAME: Jaime

FUTURE PLANS: Driving my coworkers crazy with my humming

BAD BABY
EARLY WARNING SIGN #56

Baby insists neighbor's
dog is real father.

"Hey, Mom, you think I could have a little service over here?"

NAME: Isabel

FUTURE PLANS: Demonstrating that nighttime is the right time to be with the one you love

"We've got some heavy precipitation in my Huggies, but I remain cautiously optimistic about a diaper change. Back to you, Bob!"

NAME: Scott

FUTURE PLANS: Meeting good-looking female anchors

"You--you don't know the first thing about washing a baby!"

NAME: Marina

FUTURE PLANS: Finding the fastest and cheapest path to spirituality

BAD BABY
EARLY WARNING SIGN #339

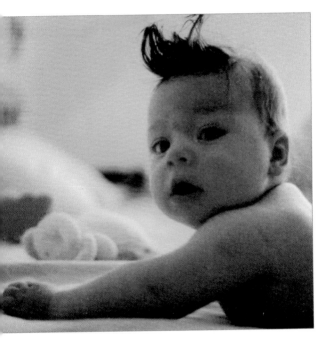

Baby does uncanny Elvis impersonation before he's two months old.

"I'm gonna nurse forever."

NAME: Sophie

FUTURE PLANS: Nurse forever

"Mom? Dad? I've decided to terminate your contract as my parents."

NAME: Elisha
FUTURE PLANS: Refusing to get rid of my antique dog-bowl collection

BAD BABY
EARLY WARNING SIGN #307

Baby believes Teletubbies
mobile is spiritual
leader.

DAILY AFFIRMATION

"Today I will stop
obsessing about my next
meal."

--Dayle

"As soon as I towel off,
baby, let's you and me
take a nap."

NAME: Nicholas

FUTURE PLANS: Appearing in
a reality show about
flatulence

"These Harley-Davidson virtual reality goggles are bitchin'."

NAME: Evelyn
FUTURE PLANS: Tearing up Yellowstone with my snowmobile

BAD BABY
EARLY WARNING SIGN #167

Baby uses fake ID to crash two-for-one bottle night.

"So that's what's been giving me gas."

NAME: Dennis

FUTURE PLANS: Reading voraciously with very little comprehension

"About your problem with the sitter . . . Joey 'Sippy Cup' will handle it."

NAME: Molly

FUTURE PLANS: Ratting out my mother

"The strained peas are kickin' in."

NAME: Ben

FUTURE PLANS: Creating a New Age religion centered on sacred bowel movements

VINTAGE BAD BABY

In 1930, Jo Anne Bigelow claims to have had vision that led to Absolut Vodka ad campaign.

BAD BABY
EARLY WARNING SIGN #58

Baby schemes with cousin
to thwart grandmother's
attempts to feed them
her special macaroni-
and-trout casserole.

"You will live a long and healthy life. You will change many diapers. In fifteen years, you will buy me a car."

NAME: Yvonne

FUTURE PLANS: Hypnotizing my college professors

"What in God's name were you thinking when you named me Evian?"

NAME: Evian
FUTURE PLANS: Changing my name

BAD BABY
EARLY WARNING SIGN #244

Baby will eat only if fed
fresh chum.

"Hmmm. That's an interesting offer, but I think I'll stay awake."

NAME: Michael

FUTURE PLANS: Avoiding tarragon and fennel

VINTAGE BAD BABY

"All the men in my family wear dresses. What about it?"

NAME: Gary

FUTURE PLANS: Starting a book club for metrosexuals

"Mommy, the doll called
me a butthead again!"

NAME: Hudson

FUTURE PLANS: Promoting the
consumption of hot cereal

DAILY AFFIRMATION

"Today I will stop being
shocked by what I find
in Mommy's drawer."

--Kayla

"Tell me you have mixers!"

NAME: Izzy

FUTURE PLANS: Knitting dickies

"I'll be right back, Dad--
I'm just taking Abby to
the dump."

NAMES: Abby and Ruby
FUTURE PLANS: Singing along
as if I know the lyrics;
biting people long after
it loses its charm

DALLAS--
Marcus "The Tongue"
Tomachevsky wreaks havoc
at stamp collectors'
convention.

"Believe me, it works
a lot better than
Miracle-Gro."

NAME: Vera

FUTURE PLANS: Giving new
meaning to term
"superfreak"

BAD BABY
EARLY WARNING SIGN #156

Baby makes unwanted
advances after naptime.

"I charge a nickel for one booger, three for a dime."

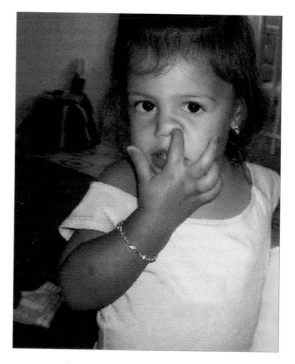

NAME: Ava

FUTURE PLANS: Opening an organic bakery

"I'm begging you--no more 'Wheels on the Bus.'"

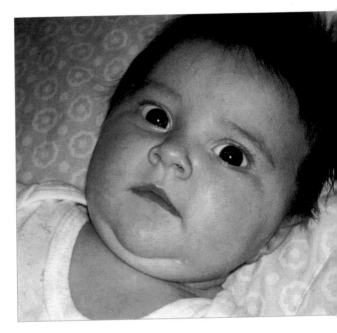

NAME: Sara
FUTURE PLANS: Liking men who change jobs frequently

BAD BABY
EARLY WARNING SIGN #333

Baby bores visitors with endless Don Corleone impersonations.

"This one tastes like brussels sprouts."

NAME: Adam

FUTURE PLANS: Importing Ukrainian cheeses

"It's 3 A.M. and these animals won't shut up!"

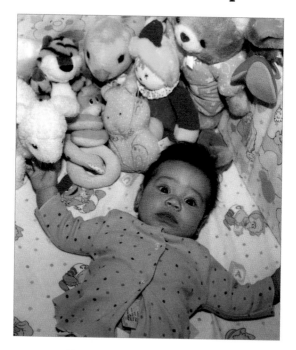

NAME: Carolina

FUTURE PLANS: Getting a single in my freshman dorm

BAD BABY
EARLY WARNING SIGN #77

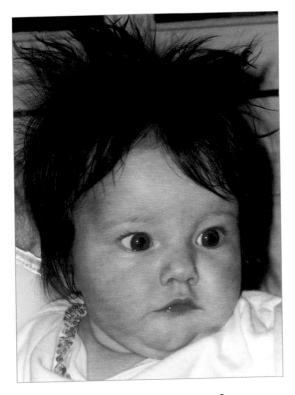

Baby's stare causes house
pets to stop eating.

"I'm not leaving the house until you put me in something less ridiculous."

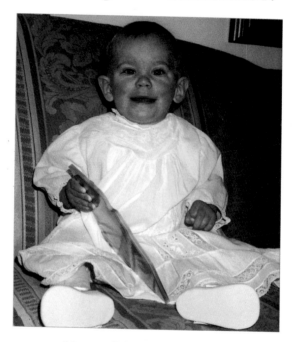

NAME: Meredith

FUTURE PLANS: Outlawing genealogy

"I have no idea what it is, but I think I've had enough."

NAME: Isabel
FUTURE PLANS: Traveling through Wisconsin on a dollar a day

BAD BABY
EARLY WARNING SIGN #100

Baby feigns food poisoning
to get better entrée.

"Bedtime? Nope, don't want to hear about it. Lalalalalala. I can't hear you."

NAME: Amanda

FUTURE PLANS: Wasting thousands of dollars on salsa lessons

BAD BABY
EARLY WARNING SIGN #501

Baby refuses to dive for
loose balls.

"You want my advice, Sid?
Lose the flowered bib."

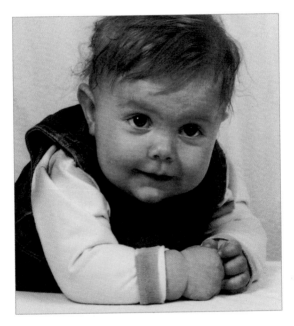

NAME: Jamie
FUTURE PLANS: Hosting
Tanning with Celebrities
on the E! channel

VINTAGE BAD BABY

"Mumsy, dear, bring me more talc for my bum."

NAME: Brewster

FUTURE PLANS: Pulling out of the stock market in early 1929

"I just told him he was adopted."

NAMES: Isabella and Joe
FUTURE PLANS: Never reading a single word of Henry James; starting a chain of Henry James literary fitness clubs

"Mom! Santa smells like a rum and coke!"

NAMES: Mark and Adam

FUTURE PLANS: Spending two weeks alone in a Denver motel room; never ordering a single thing from L.L. Bean

"Tofutti makes me puke."

NAME: Clara

FUTURE PLANS: Making my own children eat spelt

"You know, Dad, you're about twenty pounds past that Speedo."

NAME: Sophia

FUTURE PLANS: Staying away from Cancun

"Whenever I see a blank wall I can't get the cap off fast enough."

NAME: Sandy

FUTURE PLANS: Haunting discount stationery stores

"Everybody out of the pool while I'm doing my business!"

NAME: Lisa

FUTURE PLANS: Owning several SUVs

"Taste this one. You won't be sorry."

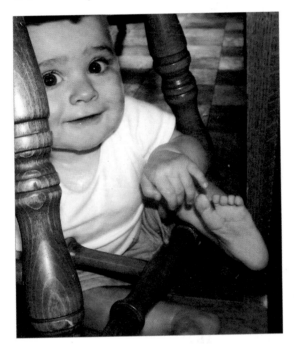

NAME: John

FUTURE PLANS: Creating my own line of spicy condiments

About the Authors

R. D. Rosen's career as a humorist spans "The Generic News" on PBS, "Saturday Night Live," and HBO's "Not Necessarily The News." He is also an Edgar Award-winning mystery novelist and the author of a forthcoming nonfiction book about one American buffalo.

Harry Prichett has written and performed for the improv comedy group Chicago City Limits, created the off-off-Broadway one-man show *Work=Pain=Success*, and is the voice you hear on numerous television and radio commercials.

Rob Battles, a senior executive for a television entertainment company, flosses daily. He's written for John Cleese (okay, once), newspapers, magazines (many now defunct), and tabloid television—but never, ever merely for pleasure.

Together, they wrote *The New York Times* bestsellers *Bad Dog* and (with Jim Edgar) *Bad Cat*. They have fathered six impeccable children.

Is Your Baby Bad Enough?

We're looking for a few bad babies to appear in a future *Bad Baby* calendar or book. If you have a photo of your precious bundle of joy looking a little less than angelic, we want it! It might even be a photo of yourself as a "vintage" bad baby.

SEND YOUR PHOTO AND FORMS TO:

Is Your Baby Bad Enough?
Workman Publishing
Grand Central Station
P.O. Box 3927
New York, NY 10163

E-MAIL YOUR DIGITAL PHOTO TO:

photo.dept@workman.com
(type "bad baby" on subject line)

BAD BABY ENTRY FORM

Baby's Name:

Parent's Name:

Street Address:

City/State/Zip:

Phone Number:

E-mail Address:

I confirm that I am the parent or guardian of the child whose photo is attached, and that I am the owner of all rights, including copyright, to the attached photo. I have also read and agreed to the rules outlined below.

Signature   245

RULES

PLEASE TAPE (<u>DO NOT STAPLE</u>) this
filled-out entry form to the back of each
photo you submit. PHOTOS NOT ACCOMPANIED BY
INDIVIDUAL ENTRY FORMS WILL NOT BE CONSIDERED.

PLEASE NOTE: The parent or guardian must
sign the entry form. If two or more children
are in the photo, please provide names and
ages for all. If the children have different
parents and/or guardians, please provide
additional consent forms.

PICTURE SIZE: The picture can be standard
snapshot size or larger and must be in sharp
focus. Adults should not be visible. Do not
fold the photo. Although we prefer snapshots,
digital images are also accepted. They should
be 300 dpi, at least 900 by 900 pixels, and be
accompanied by black-and-white or color print-
outs with entry forms attached. Children
should live in North America (or in a territory
or protectorate of the United States, or on a
United States military base).

Photos will be selected by our panel of Bad
Baby Judges, which may include Workman
Publishing Company staff. The authors reserve
the right to change a baby's name to avoid
duplication or better suit a caption, and to
ascribe to the baby fictional characteristics
and preferences.

Photos submitted become the property of
Workman Publishing, which will have the
right, without further consideration, to use
the photos in *Bad Baby*, and in any other
calendar, book, publication, media, and
promotion.